# SHIMMER and SHINE

# AWESOME ANIMALS DIVINE!

## A Guide to Creatures Around the World

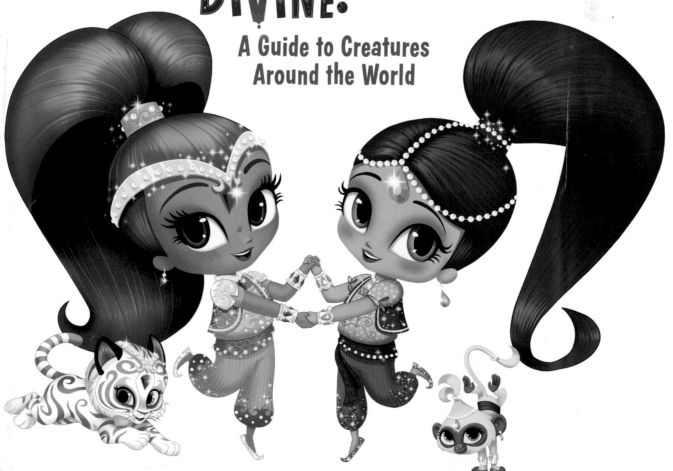

Animals are so interesting! I wish we could go on an animal adventure.

2

Boom Zahramay,
first wish of the day!
Shimmer and Shine,
animal adventure divine!

3

# River Otters

## Underwater acrobats!

River otters love to play in the water! They like to glide on their bellies and do somersaults. They're native to North America and live around rivers, streams and lakes.

Otters sure know how to have a good time!

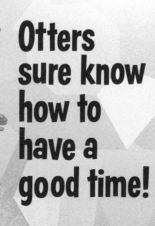

**Did you know?**

These creatures can stay underwater for up to four minutes.

# Butterflies

## Take flight!

Butterflies start out as caterpillars! They go through a special process where they build cocoons, grow wings and become butterflies.

Caterpillars transform into butterflies... like magic!

**Did you know?** Butterflies live everywhere except Antarctica!

# Cottontail Rabbits

## Everybunny hop to it!

Cottontail rabbits are found all over the United States! Rabbits are herbivores, which means they only eat plants.

**HERBIVORE**
is pronounced
**erb-uh-vor**

Awww, look at that cute fluffy tail!

# Bottlenose Dolphins

## Dolphins divine!

Dolphins are aquatic mammals. That means they need to come up to the surface for air. They breathe through blowholes on the tops of their heads!

**Did you know?**

A group of dolphins is called a school.

Dolphins can jump up to 20 feet high—that's as high as a giraffe is tall!

11

# Macaws

## Spread your wings and fly!

Macaws are an extra colorful kind of parrot. They have super strong beaks for cracking nuts and seeds.

Wow! So many beautiful colors!

**Did you know?**
Macaws are really loud. They communicate with lots of different calls, squawks and screams!

# Giant Pandas

## Pandas rock!

Giant pandas are cuddly looking bears that eat a lot of bamboo. A whole lot. They'll spend 12 hours a day just chomping on bamboo! Luckily, their broad, flat teeth are perfect for maximum bamboo consumption!

All this talk about eating is making me hungry. But I think I'd rather have Gooey Gummy Genie Jelly than bamboo!

**Did you know?** Pandas are really shy! They stay far away from areas with people.

# Hedgehogs

## Pretty prickly!

Hedgehogs are super cute to look at, but don't touch! Their bodies are covered in prickly spines meant to protect them. When they curl up, they become spiky balls.

**Did you know?**

Baby hedgehogs are called hoglets!

Hedgehogs are zahramazing!

# Little Penguins

## Feather friends!

These tiny birds are also called Little Blue penguins or Fairy penguins! They're the smallest species of penguin in the world. Little penguins mostly live in Australia and New Zealand.

Little Penguins? I LOVE Little Penguins!

## Did you know?

Penguins are great swimmers. They are birds but they don't fly in the air... they "fly" underwater by using their wings as flippers!

# Panther Chameleons

## Incredible colors!

Panther chameleons are some of the most colorful reptiles, thanks to their awesome scales. Most chameleons only change from brown to green, but panther chameleons can turn all sorts of bright colors!

Oh, my genie! It's an animal that can turn every color of the rainbow!

## Sound It Out
**CHAMELEON**
is pronounced
ka-meel-ee-on

# Peacocks

## Make it shimmer and shine!

Peacocks like to fan out their really big, colorful, iridescent tail feathers. Male peacocks use their pretty tails to impress female peahens!

I love their feathers!

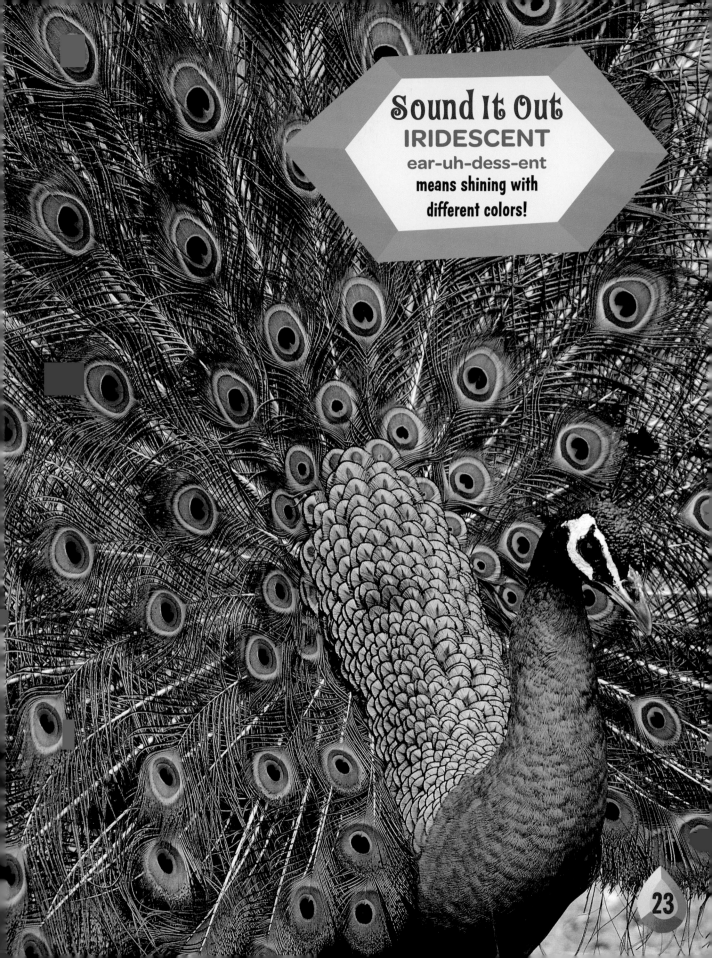

**Sound It Out**
**IRIDESCENT**
ear-uh-dess-ent
means shining with
different colors!

23

# Capuchin Monkeys

## Talented tails!

Capuchin monkeys are one of the smartest species of monkey. They love to discover new things and can even learn how to use tools!

# Did you know?

Most monkeys have long tails that they can use like extra arms!

These guys love to monkey around, just like you, Tala!

# Tigers

## So many stripes!

Tigers are the largest cats in the world! They can weigh more than 700 pounds. They also have more than 100 stripes!

I love their stripes—but my favorite tiger stripes are yours, Nahal!

**Did you know?**
Most cats don't like water, but tigers love it! They're super strong swimmers.

# Arctic Foxes

## SNOW adorable!

An Arctic fox's fur is more than just warm and pretty to look at—it's camouflage! A white coat helps the fox blend into its snowy environment.

An Arctic fox's coat changes color, just like yours, Parisa! When the season changes, the Arctic fox's coat turns brown-grey.

## Sound It Out

**CAMOUFLAGE**
is pronounced
**kam-oh-flahj**

Feathers, fins and fascinating features
We loved learning about
these incredible creatures!

With magical powers
that shimmer and shine
Boom Zahramay!
We'll see you next time!

**Media Lab Books**
**For inquiries, call 646-838-6637**

Copyright 2017 Topix Media Lab

Published by Topix Media Lab
14 Wall Street, Suite 4B
New York, NY 10005

Printed in China

ISBN-10: 1-942556-80-2
ISBN-13: 978-1-942556-80-0

**CEO** Tony Romando

**Vice President of Brand Marketing** Joy Bomba
**Director of Finance** Vandana Patel
**Director of Sales and New Markets** Tom Mifsud
**Manufacturing Director** Nancy Puskuldjian
**Financial Analyst** Matthew Quinn
**Brand Marketing Assistant** Taylor Hamilton

**Editor-in-Chief** Jeff Ashworth
**Creative Director** Steven Charny
**Photo Director** Dave Weiss
**Managing Editor** Courtney Kerrigan
**Senior Editors** Tim Baker, James Ellis

**Content Editor** Kaytie Norman
**Content Designer** Rebecca Stone
**Content Photo Editor** Catherine Armanasco
**Art Director** Susan Dazzo
**Assistant Managing Editor** Holland Baker
**Senior Designer** Michelle Lock
**Designer** Danielle Santucci
**Assistant Photo Editor** Jessica Ariel Wendroff
**Assistant Editors** Trevor Courneen, Alicia Kort
**Editorial Assistant** Isabella Torchia

**Co-Founders** Bob Lee, Tony Romando

1C G17 1